Life Isn't Always a
Bowl of Cherries

Sireana Thompson

© Sireana Thompson.

All rights reserved. This book or any portion thereof may not be reproduced or used in any manner whatsoever without the express written permission of the publisher except for the use of brief quotations in a book review.

ISBN: 978-1-66783-733-8

CONTENTS

The Beginning 1

The Dormitory 5

Gallup, New Mexico 13

Brown School 15

Patterdale 27

Back Home in Dulce 33

Life on the Street 40

A New Beginning 47

R.T. 55

THE BEGINNING

My name is Sireana Ivylay Thompson. My nickname is Bree, which was given to me by my cousin. I also have an Indian name which means small, but I don't know how to spell it. I am a Jicarilla Apache and I live on a reservation called Dulce. I live on the south side of town near to the place I grew up.

Dulce is in New Mexico, near the Colorado state line. We have one store, a post office, two gas stations, a tribal building, a casino, bar, and a community center, all in the middle of town. The Game and Fish is by the old airport. The clinic and the dormitory are on the eastside of town. There are more work places here and there I didn't write down, plus a lot of houses all over. The Dulce that I remember growing up in was a lot smaller than it is now.

Now that you know what Dulce looks like, I would like to write about my life. This is my true story, but I have changed some names to protect the privacy of those involved.

My father was a loving man. He was nice to everyone and always smiling and joking. He was in the war and worked at the Sawmill in Dulce, and did odd jobs for people. He also worked in Pagosa Springs, Colorado at a saw mill.

My mother was a kind person and a loving mother. She took care of us. I had a big family: four brothers, eight sisters, plus me. Most of my family is gone. We were raised by our parents. We lived on the reservation in Barrella, on land my dad owned. I don't really remember much because I was too small. Anyway, we lived there for a while. Later we moved into town (Dulce) and my dad got a job at the saw mill.

We lived on top of a hill above the saw mill. First we lived in a tent then later on my dad built us a house. It was a nice house. We didn't have electric so we used oil lamps. We also had a wood stove. We had an outside bathroom, and we didn't have water so we would take our buckets down to the saw mill to get water.

One time our mother sent us to go fill the water buckets, my sisters Coors, Frankie, and me. On our way home our neighbor Mae called us to her house so we left the buckets of water on top of the hill and we went down to her house. She invited us inside to eat. I guess my mother went to get the water from the hill. When we got home she was really mad. I don't think we ever went to Mae's house again.

I remember every day the whistle would blow at 5:00pm from the saw mill. My mother would say "Here comes your Dad!" We would run up to the hill to meet him and he would always have a big smile on his face. We were Laughing and happy to see him. It was something we did every day when he was working.

We also had chickens, so we grew up on fresh eggs and chicken. Sometimes my dad would kill a chicken for supper. Sometimes it would run off with no head. He would tell my sister to go get it. Sometimes it would get caught in a fence but she would bring it back and it would be our supper.

It was fun having chickens until one day there was no more chickens. I guess my dad gave them away.

I also remember this old man who had an old truck. I guess he didn't live too far up the hill from us. Every time we would be playing outside and he would go by we would wave at him. Then on his way back home he would throw candy to us. That would happen once in a while.

I remember when my parents would go to town. They would have our brother take us small ones up the hill for a walk so we didn't cry after them. Sometimes they would not come home all day. In the evening, we would sit outside and watch all the cars going by. Every time a car passed by, we would think it was them and wait to see the car turn down our road. But then it would just go by. We would sit outside until it got late then we would go inside. Then here they came. You could tell they were drunk because they would be laughing. So we would all jump into bed and act like we were sleeping.

Then my older sister started doing the same thing. She would wait until my parents left, and then she would take my other sister Coors with her. She would take my brother too, if he was home. Before they left she would have to sew my doll some clothes because I told her I would tell on her and that was the only way she would keep me from telling. But they would always come home before my parents.

I also had a half-brother named Matt. He was my dad's son. He would come home once in a while to visit. He came home several times when my parents were drunk. He didn't like to see them drunk. He would find all their wine and call them outside, and he would spill out all the wine in front of them. He would try every way to keep my parents sober but it was hard to do.

We would end up in the foster home a lot. Our brother Matt would try to get us out but they would not let him. We had to wait until our parents came to get us. I didn't like the foster home but that was the only place they could put us. Then when my sisters and brother got older, they were sent to the dorm to live so they could attend school. That left my little brother Junior and me.

We would sit on top of the hill by the house, looking down town wishing we were old enough to be in the dorm. Then it would start to get night, so we would go inside and our parents were passed out. We would open a can of spinach and eat it, and then we would crawl into bed wherever we could and go to sleep.

wherever we could and go to sleep.

One time Junior and I went to town with our parents. My parents got drunk on us, so we ended up sitting behind the old trailer park. Then, here comes my Grandma with my aunt and her kids. My Grandma saw that my parents were all drunk. She got after them and told them she was taking Junior and me home with her.

Junior would not go, so we left him with my parents. I got in the car and we started going to Barrella, that's where my grandma lived, in a one room house. When we got there my grandma told me to get some wood from outside. I got the wood and she made supper. She made me a bed by her so I could go to sleep. The next day I was sitting on the porch. My grandma happened to look down the ditch on the other side of the road. She said "Look who's coming". I saw my mom and dad, and my little brother was on my dad's shoulders. I just sat there on the porch looking at them. They were sober so after that we went home.

THE DORMITORY

When I was five or six years old, I went to the dorm also. It was ok but you had to do chores and work in the dining room. It looked like I would always have pots and pans. But I never complained I just did my work. School was from 8:00am to 3:00pm, then we would go back to the dorm, watch TV, then go to supper. After supper was study hour, then free time until bed time.

Right before I had moved into the dorm, my brother Matt had died.

One night, I was laying in my bed at the dorm and I heard boots coming down the hall. My bed was in the room at the end of the hall by the EXIT sign. The first thing that came to my mind was my brother Matt coming down the hall. I got so scared that I jumped on the table between my cousin Biz's bed and mine. Her bed was on the top bunk. She woke up and said "What's wrong?" I said "He's coming". She said "Who?" I said "my brother". We both got scared and jumped under the covers. Then she peeked out and said "He is sitting at the foot of the bed". So we stayed under the covers until the lights came on. Then I went back to my bed.

My sister Frankie was also in the dorm, but when we told her about seeing my brother, she said she had not seen or heard anything, so we just forgot about it.

My parents would come to the dorm to check us out for the weekend. Sometimes I couldn't go home because I was sick. I don't know why but when I was little, I used to get sick a lot.

I remember this one time they came to check us out but I had to stay because I was sick, so I started crying, looking out the window watching them walk away. I guess they came back and gave the dorm matron a doll to give to me. I named her Matilda. I had that doll for a very long time.

One time I had the German measles. There was another girl sick with the measles so they put us in a room where nobody could get near us. It was during Christmas and I didn't get to go home. One night I was dreaming there was big dough on me. I guess I was moving my hands and arms to keep that big dough away from me. When I woke up the girl was sure looking at me. She asked me what I was doing. We were just laughing about it. We stayed in that room until we got better.

One time my sister Frankie and her friends were playing the Ouija board. I happened to be there so I told them to tell the Ouija board that if it is real, give them a sign and shake the bed. While they were concentrating, I crawled under the bed and grabbed the bed springs and started shaking the bed with them on it. They all got scared and threw the Ouija board and started running down the hallway screaming! I started laughing and they all got mad at me. But we all laughed about it. I never did it again, but it was funny.

One time after study hour Frankie and I were sure yelling dirty words to these two guys going back to their dorm. We were sure yelling out the window and we did not hear the matron coming down the hall. She took both of us to the bathroom and told us to wash our mouth out with soap. She stood there and watched us to make sure we did it. We did, and it tasted awful. That was no fun. We never yelled dirty words out the window again.

When I was around nine years old, our parents took us out of the dorm for a while, and we went to school from home. It did not last long before we were back in the dorm. I remember coming home after school one day with my two sisters and my little brother, and my mother was making fry bread when we went inside. She gave us each a piece to eat. When I was eating mine I tasted a bandage, so I told my mother "mine tastes like bandage". She got mad and told me "No it does not!" So I pulled out a bandage from my mouth. I told her "See!" and we all started laughing.

After that we all went outside to play. Nobody wanted to play with me so I went inside and told my mother. She told me to stay inside and to look under the mattress. I lifted up the mattress and there were pops and candies under it. She told me to get a pop and candy but to drink and eat the candy inside. I don't know why my sisters and little brother didn't like to play with me. I guess I was too mean. I would always end up playing by myself. I had a Mickey Mouse record player and I used to always play my favorite record on it which was Jeannie C. Riley. My favorite song was "Run Jennie Run". Every night I would lay on my bed and sing to it. My mother use to tell me "Turn off that record player and throw your gum away and go to sleep".

Then later on I liked to sing it wherever I was going. I didn't know my little brother liked that song. He used to tell me to sing it again and I would. I don't know what ever happened to that record.

My mother was a good mother. One time she made my sister Frankie and I bags out of Clorox bottles. They came out nice. Another time when nobody wanted to play with me my mother made me some rag dolls. Then I went outside and played under the porch by myself. She would always find a way to make me happy.

Then one time my parents took us out of the dorm for the summer. We went out to these peoples' land where my dad could take care of their sheep. We lived in a tent. We got to ride horses. One time my sister Coors and I were riding Big Red. He was an old horse we used to laugh about because when he would go up the hill, he would always let out gas. We went to go check on the sheep. We were going up the ditch when I slipped off the back of the horse. My sister saw me standing by the horse and said "what happened?" I told her I slid off the back of the horse. We were laughing about it. So I got back on and we rode Big Red back to the tent. Then it was my little brother's and my turn. We asked our dad if we could take Big Red to drink some water and he said OK. So we started riding him to the pond. I had a stick so I told my little brother "I'm going to whip him so he can run". I swiped him and he put his butt up. We got scared and got off him and let him go on his own. We walked back to the camp and my dad said "Where is the horse?" We told him what happened and he told us to go and get the horse. He was on the other side of the hill. We didn't want to but we went anyway. Our older brother caught him and took him back to the camp. My little brother and I never rode Big Red again.

It was fun living out in the woods but I used to always get mad at my dad because every time it was time to wash the dishes he would always say "Sireana you wash dishes". My sisters and little brother always got to go and play. I asked my dad how come I have to always wash dishes and those guys get to go play. He said "because when you grow up I don't want you to be lazy". Then I understood why I always washed dishes.

It was fun being at camp but we had to go back to the dorm to go back to school.

Sometimes on holidays my parents didn't come to get us out of the dorm. My sisters Coors and Frankie got checked out by someone else, and my little brother would go with Frankie. Me, I would end up going with anybody who would take me. Sometimes I would end up staying in the dorm which was ok.

Another time when we were out of the dorm for the summer my dad was working in Pagosa Springs, Colorado. He was working at a sawmill for man named Jim who had 2 kids, Sue and Timmy. They were about our age and sometimes we had fun playing with them on the miniature golf course.

We used to go to church on Sundays. My sister Coors, Frankie and I all had the same dresses but different colors. Every time after church we had to change our clothes and hang our dresses in the closet until next Sunday. My mother always liked to dress us the same and put ribbons in our hair. I think she wished she had twins.

Then one day my dad made this rule that if you don't get up for breakfast you don't eat. But when I got up my mom used to tell me to be quiet and she would come close the door to the bedroom and give me my breakfast. I never said anything to anyone. After summer, it was back to the dorm.

This one time when I was about 11 years old, this girl that was older than me told me to meet her by the gym after school. I said OK and I went to meet her. She had a gas can with her and I asked her what it was. I think she told me it was gas. I asked her how you get high from it. She gave me a rag and told me to sniff it until I get a buzz. I guess I did not hear her right, I thought she said when you hear a buzz. So I kept trying to listen for a buzz. But I did get high because the next thing I knew we were both sitting on the porch sniffing. I looked at her and she looked like she was going round and round and I was going back and forth. I told her what we were doing and we couldn't stop laughing. We kept sniffing until the Matron called me inside.

When I got inside someone told me to go to the bathroom and wipe my mouth, there was something white on my mouth. So I went into the bathroom and wiped my mouth. After that, I got into sniffing. I started sniffing gas, lighter fluid and paint.

One time Frankie and I were at our cousin's house. We were sitting outside by the fence at night. We were sniffing and laughing, all of a sudden Frankie got up with her arms straight in front of her. She started coming toward me. I got scared and grabbed my cousin who was just laughing. I said "What's wrong with her?" I was so scared because she kept coming at me, so I think I slapped her and told her to stop it. Then she started walking away from us. We were standing there just looking at her walk away. She fell into a ditch and got up and said "I'm alive!" Then she started walking again. My cousin and I called her back and she turned around and asked us what happened. We told her and we all just starting laughing. She said she didn't know what happened. I think that scared us and we stopped sniffing for the night.

Then one time my two sisters and my little brother, plus our cousin and me were in the arroyo sure sniffing. Here comes our dad. He yelled at us. We all got scared and ran different ways. He called all of us. We were scared but we went to him. He told all of us he didn't want us sniffing. So we all stopped and went home.

Then one night we were with our cousin and we told him we didn't want to go back to the dorm. So, he asked his sister and her husband if we could stay with them and they said OK. That's how we ended up staying with them. They had three kids; two boys, one was a baby, and one little girl.

We went to school every day. It was OK but they had a rule: If you don't get an A in school you can't go anywhere. So I used to change my F's to A's so I could go to the center with my friends. I don't think they ever caught on to what I was doing.

Then one day my sister and I used the car. We ruined it by going on the gravel real fast. They got mad at us, but they got over it.

We used to go to Albuquerque to go see wrestling. We even got to see Charlie Pride. Coming back from Albuquerque my sister and I had to take turns driving. I didn't know how to drive but I guess I did good, because I had to drive back one time and everybody went to sleep. The only problem I had was my legs were too short and I could not touch the button on the floor to turn the lights dim when a car or truck was coming. To make it worse, it was dark. People would get mad and turn their lights back bright on me. But we all made it home safe.

This one day our guardian told us to clean out the car. When my sister and I were cleaning out the car we saw our uncle, aunt and three of their kids coming toward the car. My aunt came toward me and slapped me. I think they were all trying to grab me. I was surprised, so was my sister, because we didn't know what was going on. My sister went inside and told our guardians what was going on. He came outside and told me to go inside. I guess he talked with them. Then he came back inside and asked me if I beat up their daughter after school. I said no, because I came home right after school. We ended up going to court with them. The judge told them not to touch me again. Later I found out it was my cousins that jumped her on top of the hill. And here she blamed me.

Later on my sister and I went back to the dorm. Back at the dorm, it seems like I got worse. I was not interested in school. I would always get into some kind of trouble. One time in Mr. Horney's class I did not do my homework, so he drew a hole on the chalk board and told me to put my nose in the circle. I said no. Then he said "OK Sireana let's take a walk to the principal's office". They told me that every day after school I would have to sit in the principal's office and do my homework.

Then one day the principal asked me if I would like to go to school somewhere else. He said he would sign the papers for me to go away. I guess I was really bad that he was more than happy to send me away.

It looks like I got even worse. I started drinking and taking pills. I felt like I didn't care what happened to me.

This one time I ended up in jail and my mother was there in jail also. She told me the social worker was planning to send me away. She said she was going to talk to the social worker to see if they would change their minds about sending me away. I guess they didn't listen to her because they sent me away anyway.

GALLUP, NEW MEXICO

I was 13 years old when I ended up going to Gallup to a treatment center. A place where they try to help you with your problem. They assign you a counselor when you get there. My counselor's name was Lilly, but I never talked to her about anything.

I guess they said I was an alcoholic which I didn't understand. I was too young to understand what an alcoholic was. I thought they sent me away because I was always in trouble and not listening in school. But I guess I was wrong. So I had no choice but to stay there.

Every morning after breakfast we all would go into the living room for an AA meeting. There were old people and young people and we all would sit in the living room and listen to people talk about their problems. When it was my turn I would just say "My name is Sireana Atole and I'm an alcoholic". That's all, no more. We had these meetings every day except on weekends. On weekends we would go out on some kind of activity or watch TV, play pool, or do anything we wanted.

Then one day I ran away with this girl named Eve. We ended up down town. We didn't know what to do because we were not from there and it was scary. So we decided to go back to the treatment Center. They put us in straight Jackets and locked us up in a room with cushions all over the walls. I guess it was like that so you don't hurt yourself. We stayed in there for I don't remember how long, but they let us out. After that I started behaving myself.

Then one day they gave me a birthday party with a going away party. I think I turned 14 years old. I don't really remember. The next thing I knew they were sending me away again.

I met Mr. Edwards at the airport and he told me I was going to Texas to a place called the Brown School. When we got on the plane I was so sad I cried almost all the way to Texas. At lunch time on the plane they served us chicken in the basket. It looked so good but I couldn't eat. Mr. Edwards said "you better eat before the chicken gets cold." I was so mad I just looked at him real mean. Like that was supposed to cheer me up!

BROWN SCHOOL

When I got there I was still lonely. I just kept to myself. The girls tried to cheer me up by inviting me to do activities with them, but I would just keep to myself.

Trouble started one day when Jane came in to the room. She was a tall, big, white girl with short hair and glasses. Someone told me her name. She said something to me and we got into an argument. The next thing I knew I had her on the bed and I was getting the best of her. I guess I was choking her. The girls called the counselors and they took me to a small cell in another building. It had a mattress on the floor and a toilet with a sink connected to it. This place reminded me of the jail in Dulce. They kept me there until they decided to let me out.

Then the counselor told me they made a mistake; they should have put Jane in there instead of me.

That was not the only time I got into a fight with her. The next time was in a different room. We got into an argument; I don't remember what it was about. She threw coffee on me. I got so mad I jumped from my bed to her side of the room and grabbed her and we started fighting. The next thing I knew I was banging her head on the wall and kneeling on her face. Someone told the counselors we were fighting. So here comes the male counselor taking me to the cell again. And Jane got away with it again. They never asked me who started the fight. After that I tried to keep out of that cell because it was no fun.

When I first got to Brown School, I thought it was a real school. Then I found out it was like a mental institution. When you are new, they assign you to a girl to show you around the place. I was assigned to a girl named Betty. She was a little taller than me. She had curly brown hair, wore glasses, and had a voice like a mature lady. She acted like one too.

She showed me around. There were a lot of buildings all over the place. My building was two stories and we were on the bottom floor. Our team's name was Terrace, and Summerset was upstairs. I guess the team's name is for what level you are on. I was on Terrace because that level was for girls who had problems. Summerset was for girls who were normal, and some were kind of normal. Then the building next to us was for older ladies. Then came the dining hall. After that was another building called Big Valley. That place was for boys not really normal and older men.

On top of the hill was a place for mentally challenged kids. I forget what they called that place. On the bottom of the hill was a building they called the Annex. It was a place for normal boys.

There were also small buildings where we would go to classes. The gym was in the middle of the place on a hill. The arts and crafts building was by our building.

We would go to classes every day except on weekends. There would be activities, like a slumber party, games, watching TV. Sometimes the girls would invite their boyfriends to watch TV.

At times we also would go to movies or eat out, like at Dairy Queen, or other places.

We had meetings Monday thru Friday from 3:00pm to 4:00pm. I never talked in the meetings. I really didn't know what to talk about. They wanted me to talk about myself and would try to make me talk, but I would not. Finally, they just left me alone. Even when I had therapy meetings with Mark I would not open up about anything.

Other than that, I got along with everybody.

After the meetings we would get ready for supper. After supper we would have free time until bedtime.

One time our team had a watermelon party. After the party I was sitting in the living room. This black girl from summerset came over to where I was sitting. She was about my size, short black hair, tiny like me. Her name was Ann. Anyway, she told me "Let's go outside I want to tell you something". So I said ok and we went outside and we sat on the staircase. It was dark.

Anyway, she said "you see that guy running down the sidewalk?" I said yes. I saw a guy running down the sidewalk with yellow hair to his shoulders. White tee shirt and blue jean shorts. He was medium built. Then she said his name was Tim, but everybody called him Bud. "He said he likes you". I just said "oh" like I was not interested. He would tell her to tell me to sit with him at lunch time. I tried, but I was too shy so I stopped sitting with him.

Then one time I was sitting in the living room. This time it was upstairs, we had moved upstairs to the south side of the building. The same black girl named Ann was peeking at me from the door of summerset. I used to wonder why she kept staring at me. I thought maybe she had never seen an Indian or something. Anyway, I just ignored her.

Then one day, they moved her down to Terrace team. That's how we got to know each other and become best friends. We were the naughtiest ones there. We would wrestle with a counselor named Dan. He was a tall white guy.

One time we stole the supervisor's pop. His name was Josh. We both ran into the bathroom with the pop. He came in after us. We were laughing because some of the girls were showering and they were screaming. We didn't care. We both locked ourselves in a stall and passed the pop back and forth. Then Ann gave Josh back the pop. After that we behaved ourselves.

This one time we were supposed to have a slumber party. Of course Ann and I ruined it. We were picking on Rob. He was a counselor. He was black and had an afro, wore glasses, and was small. Anyway, Ann took his pen and he chased us down the hallway to one of the girl's rooms. One of the girls was in there changing her clothes. We didn't care; we just went in there and crawled under the beds. She acted like she didn't care either because she was just laughing. Rob didn't care either; he just wanted his pen back. Ann gave it back. We didn't have a slumber party because of us. The girls got upset but got over it.

This one time the counselors and we girls were talking about making a play. We came up with Cinderella. I was chosen to play Cinderella. My Prince Charming was Pete. He was a Spanish boy. Three of the girls played my stepsisters and the mean step mother. It was a good play, everybody liked it.

Later on I played the narrator in a different play. I could not say this one word so my counselor Bobby helped me with the word until I got it right. It was a good play too. After that we never made another play.

Then this one day I was coming back from class. The counselor May called me into the office to ask me if I wanted to go off campus with a guy named Ken. That was Bud's Buddy. So I said OK. I really didn't know what was going on. But Bud called me outside to tell me why I was going off campus with Ken. We were supposed to go get some liquor.

So I checked out and went with Ken to town. We really didn't talk because we didn't know each other. He asked me if Bud told me why we were going to town and I said yes. After that I didn't say anymore. He did all the talking. When we got to town we went to the store and he bought the liquor and we started back to the school. When we got back it was dark.

I went inside to check in. May told me Bud invited me to the Annex to watch TV and asked if I would like to go. I said OK. I started going to the Annex. When I heard someone call my name it was Bud, he was coming from the other side of the road where there were a lot of trees. He told me to go ahead and go to the party and he would meet me there. I said OK and went to the party. I sat by a girl named Clare. I guess Wade, the guy she was going with was out there drinking too because she was sitting by herself.

Every once in a while some of the guys would come inside laughing and talking to the counselors like nothing was going on. The counselors knew they were drunk but did not say anything. So Clare and I ended up watching TV by ourselves until the party was over. After the party I met Bud outside. He walked me to the bridge. We said our good nights and he went to kiss me. He stuck his tongue in my mouth.

I got scared and pushed him away. I ran back to my dorm. I guess I got scared because I did not know what he was doing. I told the girls what he did and they told me that's what they call "French kissing" which I had never heard of. After that Bud never tried to kiss me again.

I guess the next day Bud and the rest of the guys were all sick. After that I went with Bud off and on. I also went with other guys, but I would always end up with Bud.

Later on, he started acting like he owned me. One time he got this little guy to spy on me. I think his name was Gilbert. He was as short as me and small built, white. Anyway one day I was leaving the dining hall. Gilbert said something to me. I chased him from the dining hall to the bridge. Then I caught him at the bridge and grabbed him by the shoulders and threw him against the bridge. I think when I threw him against the bridge he hit hard because he made some kind of sound. I got scared and asked him if he was ok. I guess he was surprised because of what I did to him. He looked at me like he was in shock and took off running. After that, every time he would see me he would go the other way.

Then there was this one guy named Fred. He was black and had a big afro. He always dressed like an African with those shirts Africans wear. He told this girl named Sue that he liked me. So one day Sue introduced me to him. He was ok at first. Then he started saying all these crazy things to me, like how much he loves me, and if I would marry him he would take me to Africa and show me around. I thought he was crazy. He lived in a make-believe world.

I would listen to him talk crazy. But afterwards he started getting to me; I could not take it anymore. I tried to ignore him but it was hard to do. Every time after lunch and supper he would be waiting for me outside. He would tell me "I love you" in front of everybody. I used to get so mad. I would tell him "I don't like you". He kept it up for a while, and then he stopped. I was glad when he stopped.

This one day I went to English class. This one boy named Wade was sitting by me. He was white, kind of chubby and short, but very nice and funny. Anyway, we started talking and he asked me if I wanted to be blood brother and sister. I said OK so he stuck our fingers with a needle and we rubbed fingers, then we became blood brother and sister. After class he told me he would walk me to my next class which was arts and crafts. We talked on our way and he told me how he liked me. But I told him I just wanted to be friends, so he said ok. We were supposed to be blood brother and sister. He is not supposed to try and go with me. How stupid.

Anyway we got to my class. Then out of nowhere here comes somebody with a stick. It was Bud. He ran by me and started hitting Wade with the stick. I got scared and felt sorry for Wade but I could not help him. I was scared Bud would hit me with the stick. Anyway, the teacher came out and stopped Bud, and Wade got away. Then everybody went to class.

After that happened, every time I would see Wade I would try to talk to him but he would tell me he couldn't talk to me anymore because of Bud. Bud told him to keep away from me. So that was the end of Wade and me being blood brother and sister. Enough of Bud.

This one day Darla came to me and Ann, and told us that Joy, Sandy, and Dora said that we were talking about them so they wanted to fight us. We didn't even know who they were because they were on Summerset side and we were on Terrace. So we tried to stay away from them. Every time we would see them we would go the other way.

Then one day Darla said "we can't show them we are chicken". So after lunch we were walking back to our building and there they were, waiting for us.

We walked up to them, and then Sandy said they were going to fight us. She said that Dora was going to fight Darla, Joy was going to fight Ann, and Sandy was going to fight me. I looked at her and I got scared. I thought to myself "how am I going to fight this big black girl?" She was probably 6 feet tall and was built like a mean, black lady. She could just grab me and throw me around like a rag doll since I was so small.

We were glad when our counselor Barb came out and told us to go inside. Darla and I went in. Of course Ann was still running her mouth. She was so funny. She was one of those little black girls that like to run their mouth and don't care about anything. Barb took us into the office and asked us why those girls wanted to fight us. We told her we did not know. So the supervisor Josh came over to see what was going on. We told him the same thing we had told Barb; we didn't know why those girls wanted to fight us.

So Josh took us to summerset to talk with Joy, Sandy and Dora. We talked to them and got everything straightened out. Then later on we all became friends.

This one day I went to town with Joy and Marlene and we went to the City Park. There was a small store across from the park that sold liquor. They wanted to drink some beer. They asked me and I said OK. So we talked about it and since Marlene was the tallest and looked like a lady she went inside to get it. She came out with a six pack of Coors.

Then we went across the street to the Park. We sat at a table and started drinking the beer. There was a couple smoking weed by us. Marlene went over to them and bought a joint from them. That was the first time I had smoked weed. They were showing me how to smoke it. I guess I got pretty high because they told me on the way back to the school I was really laughing to myself.

When we got back to the school they told me to go straight in and they would sign me in. They said if anyone asked me why my eyes were red to tell them I was tired. Nobody noticed me but Ann asked me why my eyes were red. I told her I was sleepy. I think she knew I was high but didn't say anything. We never got caught which was good.

Then one day I was going back to my dorm, not thinking about anything. When I got to the dorm I saw the therapist Mark and the counselors talking in the office. I went to the living room and sat down. The counselor called me into the office and told me Mark wanted to see me in his office. His office was downstairs so I went to his office.

He was sitting behind his desk, so I sat on a chair. Then he told me I lost my mother. I just started crying and ran upstairs to my room. The girls tried to comfort me but I kept crying.

The next day they put me on a plane back to Dulce.

I stayed at my sister's house until everything was over. Then I went back to Texas. Back to the Brown School. Doing everything over again. Go to meetings. Go to classes.

One day I came out of class and Walter happens to be around. He is a black boy built with a lot of muscles. We went together for a while but it didn't work out so we just became friends.

Anyway, we were standing there talking, I forget what we were talking about. All of a sudden I wanted to move my leg, and then I felt something heavy under my shoe. I was hoping Walter would stop talking and leave so I could see what was under my shoe. He finally left. So I sat down on the wall. I looked under my shoe there it was, a

23

rock. The kind of shoes I had on were like the kind Elton John would wear. I took it out and started laughing, then I started walking back to my dorm.

Then one day the therapist and counselor told me my sister was coming to visit me for thanksgiving. When I saw her I was happy to see her. She was a little chubby, but besides that we had a great time. I was supposed to take her to the cafeteria for thanksgiving dinner. Instead I took her to town for a hamburger. I guess she didn't mind because she didn't complain. I guess they let her visit me so she could talk to me and help me open up more with my problems. It didn't work because all we did was have fun all the time she was there with me.

Then it was time for her to leave. When she left I got all lonely again but I got over it.

I wanted to go to school where she was but she told me not to because I would not like it. So I just forgot about it and continued my everyday doings, going to classes and meetings.

Then one day I came back from classes and Mark and the counselors were in the office. They called me in there. They were trying to make me talk but I would not. The next thing I knew they got me on the floor and they were sitting on me making me scream and cry. They would not get off me until I stopped screaming. They started doing that to me to get me to open up but it seemed not to work. They tried every way but they couldn't get me to open up. Other than that I had fun days. Like the time we went to San Antonio to Six Flags. It was a big place with lots of rides. Ann, Jill and I rode the roller coaster. It was a big one. I don't know how many times we rode it. I had a great time that day.

The next time was when we went to Corpus Christie, Texas. It was a lot of fun. We camped out for two weeks. We played Frisbee and the counselors took a lot of pictures of us. One day I went fishing with Don, one of our counselors. We were in the ocean. He told me "you got one" so I started pulling in my rod. I looked at it. It was not a fish it was something else. I got scared and threw my rod in the water and screamed and started running back to shore. So Don pulled it in and it was a sting ray which I had never seen before. He said the tail was poison, if it stings you it can kill you. I guess he cut it off and put it back in the ocean. After that I didn't want to fish anymore. Other than that, I enjoyed myself at the ocean.

Even though I had a lot of fun I was still naughty. One night we were having study hour. Nora, Ann and I wrote notes to each other to run away. So we ran away at night. I remember getting as far as a small town outside of New Orleans. We got in a car with a white man and he bought us some hamburgers and a case of beer, which was a mistake. I guess I got drunk and don't remember anything that happened. When I came to I was in New Orleans with Ann. I asked her where Nora was, and she said she had kept going; she was going to her home. We ended up going to Ann's brother's house. His name was Bob and he had a wife named Jessie, and a baby. Bob and his friend LaLa wanted me to make money on the streets for them, which I knew nothing about. Ann and I were scared. I think she told me she was sorry she took me to his house. The next day I guess her mother found out about us. She went over there and took as away from there.

We ended up going with Ann's other brother Rick and his friend Paul. We stayed in the horse stable with them. We stayed there with them until her mother came up with some money to put us on the bus. It seems like we were there about two weeks, then Ann's mother came for u s and made sure we got on the bus.

When we got on the bus we met this white guy who had some weed. He asked us if we smoked weed, and I guess we said yes. Then he started taking the tobacco out of a cigarette and putting weed in it. Then we were all taking turns going to the restroom and taking hits. When he was getting off the bus, he gave us the bag of weed. So when we got to Austin we went to the bathroom and made a joint. We smoked it before the counselor came to pick us up. I think Ann threw the rest away.

I guess it got me high because when we got back to the dorm we had a meeting and our eyes were real red. I think they put me in the cell. Don came to talk to me and I told him I didn't like it there and that I wanted to be with my sister in Phoenix. She wrote to me and told me not to go there because I would not like it. But I would not listen to her.

Arrangements were made for me to go to Phoenix, Arizona to where my sister was. The school was named Patterdale. I think I was 16 years old at that time.

PATTERDALE

When I got to Patterdale they put me in an inside cottage where you had to wear a uniform and the only time you could wear your own clothes was after school. It was OK at first. But the girls used to tell my sister Fran that I was mean and that I used to push them down the stairs, which I don't remember doing but I guess I did. I didn't make friends right away. I guess I was still the same person I was before: mean.

The nuns would get my sister Fran to come over to my cottage to talk to me. But of course it didn't work so all we did was just sit there laughing with each other. Fran and I had the same counselor, her name was Dora. Dora tried the same thing with me that they did at the Brown School; try to make me talk about my problems, which I still didn't know anything about. I felt like I didn't have any problems, I really didn't know what they wanted out of me. So I would end up sitting on the patio a lot, which didn't do me any good.

I got along with some of the girls and also some of the nuns, and the Aunts too. You had to call them "Aunts" and "Uncles" at that school. There was really nothing to do at the school, I guess because it was a catholic school.

When they would not pressure me I would have a good time. Like this one night Mary and Donna got some snacks out of the kitchen when aunt Margaret was working. I guess they put an apple under my pillow, which I didn't know anything about. I went to get ready to go to bed and I pulled my covers down. Out rolled an apple and it landed right by Aunt Margaret's feet. I was surprised. I told her I didn't know anything about it. She said it was ok and I didn't get in trouble, in fact no one did.

Then one time they let my sister Fran and I go home for vacation. We didn't want to go back to Patterdale, so Rose and my other sister Cora took us to our dad out in the woods. The cops came to get us. We ran away but they caught us and put us in jail. We stayed in jail for a while. Then when they were taking us to Farmington to the airport the cop hand-cuffed us together and made sure we got on the plane.

I took some cigarettes back with me. I used to hide them under my mattress. Whenever I could I would go into the bathroom and turn on the shower to hot and smoke a cigarette. Then one day I told some of the girls and we decided to smoke that night. We all went into the bathroom. We were sure blowing the smoke in the vent, and we didn't even think that the vent went to the next cottage, where the sister's room was. I don't know if she ever smelled it.

Afterwards, we got caught so we had a meeting with sister Vell. She asked who had the cigarettes and everyone said nothing. There was this one Navajo girl, I forget her name, and she was going to say something. I looked at her like you better not say anything. So she didn't say nothing. But later on she told on me. My punishment was to keep away from everyone and eat in the broom closet and brush my teeth and shower after everyone else was finished. I didn't care even if I felt like a prisoner. But I got through it. That still didn't teach me nothing.

Life Isn't Always a Bowl of Cherries

One day I guess my Dad made arrangements for us to get out of school for a while to go visit our brother Bob and his family in Artesia. So, Fran and I got a plane to Farmington NM. There, we met our father. He was standing there waiting for us. He had a big smile on his face. We were so glad to see him waiting there. I wanted to run up and hug him. But you know us Indians, we don't do that.

We spent the night in Dulce then the next day we took the bus to Artesia, where Bobby met us at the bus station. He was still his old self. He liked to make jokes. When he picked up my purse he said you want your suitcase in the truck too? We all started laughing. I said "that's not a suitcase it's my purse".

Then we went to a movie that night. We all enjoyed it. After the movie we went to his house. He had a wife named Mary and two little boys. One was named Mac and the baby was Bobby Jr.

The next day we went to the park to play baseball. Our dad was the pitcher. He would pitch us hard balls, but we had a lot of fun. We did other things with them before we had to return back to school. We all had a great time together.

Then the sad day for me was when my sister Fran graduated from school. I went to the graduation ceremony. I listened to her speech. It made me cry. I didn't want her to go, but she had to.

Then they moved me to the outside cottage. It was no different from the inside cottages. I met a girl named June. She was fun to be around. She used to work off campus. One day she brought some cigarettes back from work. One day June, Denise and I went to the place where they grew a lot of oranges. They showed me a place where they used to sit. It looked like a hut. Anyway, we sat in there and smoked some cigarettes. When we finished we got some oranges and wiped them all over us so we would not smell like cigarettes. I guess it worked because we got away with it.

Then one day we had a festival for all the countries, where we all came dressed like a different country. We were Iran, so we had to dress like them, speak and learn about their culture. Anyway, we had a big feast where every cottage brought a different kind of food. It was fun.

I was sitting with this girl whose name I forget so I'll call her Kay. We started talking about running away. That evening after everything was over, we went back to our cottage. I told Kay to ask Sister Colleen for some toilet paper, so we could run out the door.

We ran through the field and she climbed the fence first then it was my turn. As Kay was going over her blouse and bra got caught on the fence. It was so funny but we didn't have time to laugh. I had to help her get untangled, then I climbed over. Then we were walking on the street trying to figure out where we were when this cop stopped by us and he got out of his car. I guess he was just going to ask us something. We got scared and started to run. Kay ran to the Highway and the cop ran after her and caught her. He had her behind the car. I went over there to help her. I started hitting and kicking the cop and told him to let her go. He let her go and we both started running again. He shouted "All I wanted was to ask you if you had seen two girls that ran away from Potterdale?" But we didn't stop, we just kept on running.

We heard this girl yelling at us telling us "come here! Come here!" she said "get inside!" So we went into her house. She asked us if we were the runaways from Patterdale, we said yes. She told us she was in Patterdale herself and how she didn't like it either. We stayed there for a while then she gave us a ride to the freeway. Then we caught a ride with these two old white guys. They took us as far as they could.

Finally, we got to Kay's house. We went to town with her brother and he showed us around. We even went to a Disco place. After that she and I went to some guy's house. She went inside and I stayed outside with some guy. He knew I was not interested in him, so we went inside and I said "let's go".

We left and went to her sister's house. Her name was Rena, her husband's name was Tom. He also had a brother named Pete. We stayed there. I guess the next day her mother made her go back to Patterdale. Rena let me stay with her and her husband and Pete. One night we were sitting in the living room and they were smoking a joint. I think I smoked some too, I don't remember. Anyway, they introduced me to their friend. His name was Dick. He was ok. He took me to the movies. Then I met Rena's little sister they called Betty. I started hanging around with her. We used to go to the Disco. We were not old enough but we would get in. I stayed with them for a while then my counselor came up there and picked me up and took me back to Patterdale.

When I got back to Patterdale they left me in the hall by myself, so I went for the door and ran away again. I went back to Chandler Arizona. This time I didn't last long. My counselor Dora came to pick me up again.

I think it was about this time that they all gave up on me. They put me in the last cottage where you stay until they decide what to do with you. So they decided to send me home. When I was leaving, this lady named Aunt Carla took me to the airport. She told me if I didn't like it when I got home to call her and she would send me a ticket to go live with her. I said OK, but the sad part is I lost her phone number! I wish I had never lost that number.

BACK HOME IN DULCE

When I came back to Dulce, I had no place to go so I went to my cousin's house.

He was sitting outside in the dark. I went over to him and asked him if I could stay with him. At first, he didn't recognize me. I told him I was Sireana. He was so happy to see me he said lets go ask my mom. So we went inside and he asked his mom and she didn't know who I was. He told her "it's Sireana" she said Oh! Then she recognized me and said it was ok. So I stayed with them and he and his sister gave me the nick-name Bree and started calling me their little sister, which a lot of people believed. It took them awhile to realize who I was.

Then I started drinking and going my way. I felt I was not welcome any more so I moved on.

I had no place to stay so I would just stay here and there. Then I started hanging out with guys. Some were married. I started hanging out with them because they would buy the booze and they were just guys to hang out with, to drink and have a good time with. Plus they liked me I guess. Well, when you have no place to go you do anything to get what you want.

Then their wives started finding out about me. Boy did they hate me and label me real good. Like one lady used to call me Miss Hollywood. She used to work at the store. Then there were ladies that jumped me for guys they were not even married to. To me they were doing the same thing I was doing, messing with married men.

I had a hard time with a lot of women not just married ones. Some that were not married. They would say all kinds of things to me. I guess it was my pretty face that got me in a lot of trouble. Plus the way I used to dress. They just could not stand me. It was like I was the worst person around. They would call me all kinds of names, any bad word you call a lady, that was me. I guess it really didn't bother me because I was still doing what I was doing. I few times I got so drunk that I jumped out of this one guys car. He would call the cops to throw me in jail. I would wake up in jail and wonder what happened to my face. It would be black and blue. I don't know how many times I did this and why. Maybe because I didn't like living, or just to do it. I don't know. When you drink you do anything stupid which you really don't remember doing, until you snap.

After that I started going to jail a lot, then detox and then the halfway house. I went to treatment centers, which did me no good because I would go right back to drinking again.

This one time I got stranded at Crene's bar. I asked this one guy for a ride and he said ok. We went on the dirt road toward Pagosa. We went as far as the water tank. He told me to do something and I said no. Then he told me to get off and I took the beer with me. It was late at night so I started walking. As I was walking something came up behind me. It was breathing real hard, it would get real close to me then it would stop. I don't know what it was but I sure was not looking back. I just said a little prayer and kept walking. It kept doing that until I hit the street light then it stopped. I went to my cousin's trailer and asked her if I could spend the night. She said ok so I stayed there.

The next day I walked back to Dulce. The same thing over again drinking with people. But the hate and jealousies of me kept going on and continue to this day.

This one time someone told me that my cousins were partying and they brought my name up and started calling me all kinds of names. One day I was at the casino and one of them came over to me. She was buzzed so we played for a while then we left. I told her "I heard one night you and your family were drinking and someone brought up my name and you all were saying bad things about me". She denied it but I know it was true because they can't stand me. They never liked me. But I told her to quit talking about me because I don't even talk about them. I don't have the time to talk about them.

I know it still goes on but it doesn't bother me. I used to always wonder why people hate me so much. Yes, I took some of their men. But some, I never did anything to them. They just hate me for who I am. I am not ashamed of what I did in my past life. It happened and I can't change it. But now I'm over 50 and trying to live the rest of my life better.

I can't figure out life. People act like they never did anything bad. But you know everyone knows what you did. So don't just label me. Look at yourself before you talk. That's why I don't consider anyone a friend. No such thing. I just talk to anyone who talks to me. Also never trust anyone because they will get into the gossip about you. That's all I have to say. Now back to my story.

I moved to the motel with my friend, her name was Nat but now she's gone. But anyway we stayed there in the motel. We use to party but not that much. I met a guy and he used to come over a lot and bring his friends sometimes. Later on Nat moved out so I had the room to myself. My sister Fran stayed with me. Until one night I invited my friend and his friend over and I guess his friend was kind of crazy or something. Anyway he busted the window and I had to pay for it. After that I moved to my cousin's house but it didn't work out so I moved to the dorm. They let me stay there for a while.

After that I moved in with my sister Dora and her husband. It was ok at first but then her husband started acting crazy. So I used to leave the house every day until my sister came home from work. Then one day I told her about how her husband was acting when she wasn't around. She never said anything until one day we went for a ride through Ignacio to Farmington. They were drinking and she confronted him but he denied it. But it was ok because he never touched me. Anyway she let me drink a little but not too much.

I met a guy named James at the motel. After that I used to go to my little brother's trailer and James and his friends would pick me up. Once when hanging out with James I found out he had no place to go so we hitched back to Dulce in the dark. Then it was getting morning when these Navajo guys picked us up and brought us back to Dulce. We went to Lumberton to buy some liquor, then they said they knew my brother in law and so we went to his house and we were drinking beer and whiskey. I guess I got too drunk and took my sister's pills. I ended up in the hospital. The nurse told me I had a 50-50 chance. I don't know why I took those pills I guess I just didn't like the way I was living. After I left the hospital I went home.

I really didn't have a home so I just went here and there to people's homes, stayed with whoever I could, drank a lot with people. The same thing over and over.

Then James and I went to stay with my sister Coors and my dad. When my dad met James, he didn't like him. He told him "I don't want you to ever hit my daughter". But you know when a father tells that to a guy he doesn't listen.

James and I decided to move to Santa Fe. We stayed in a motel called Kingston. I cleaned rooms and James would help with the repair of the place. It was hard to understand the owners because they were from India.

Then we moved to Court Motel.

It was a nice place, one room with a small kitchen and bathroom. James worked for the landlord and once in a while I would watch his friend's little boy. He was a big baby but I enjoyed having him around. One night we got drunk with our neighbors. James and I got into an argument. I got mad and broke this statue. It was an eagle. I started swinging it at him so he couldn't get to me. The neighbor got so scared he didn't know what to do so he just sat there and watched the whole thing. James talked me into calming down, so I put the statue down. That's when he got a hold of it and beat me up real bad. The next day I looked at myself in the mirror and my face was all black and blue. I looked terrible. Then he had the nerve to take me to a restaurant to eat out. I guess he was proud of his work. I don't remember how many times he beat me up. The last time I told him I was going to call my sister Dora and tell her what was going on. After that he left me alone.

We stayed together a little longer. One day he got his hands on some money I had and that night he took off with his friend to the bar. I couldn't go because I was not old enough and he didn't come back for a long time. So I talked to this guy. I asked him if he could get me some beer and he said ok. I went with him to the liquor store, he got me the beer, then we went to the bar to get James. But James didn't want to go. He was enjoying my money I guess. Anyway, I went back to the room. That guy and I went to the room and we were drinking a beer and talking. Nothing more. Then later on here comes James and his friend back from the bar. James came in and saw that guy sitting there talking to me and he got mad and said something to him in Spanish. The next thing I knew they were fighting with each other. I guess that guy had a knife and stabbed James in the bathroom. I saw James laying on the floor and I called his name but he didn't answer, so I went over to the neighbor's room and he helped me call the police. The ambulance came and took James to the hospital. I had to talk to the investigators and tell them what I knew, so I did that. After that I stayed in the room a little longer. My cousin and friend came over and stayed with me for a while. We went to the hospital to visit James, he looked terrible. He couldn't talk. So I kept going to visit him until one day my cousin and friend left. I stayed at the room a little longer. Then one night I was sitting in bed and I heard a knock. I looked out the curtain and it was my sister Dora, and Rosa. I opened the door for them and they came in. I told them I was by myself, that James got stabbed and was in the hospital. After that I went home with them. As always, I had no place to go so I just stayed here and there until one time I was drinking at the bar. My cousin Ann asked me where I was staying and I told her nowhere, so she asked me if I would like to stay with her. It was ok for a while. She stayed at her mom's with her kids, one girl and two boys. We all slept in one room.

Then one morning everyone was in the living room crying. I got up and asked Ann why everyone was crying. She said "my uncle passed away" and I said "who?" She said "your dad". I looked at her and yelled "not my dad" and broke up in tears. She just grabbed me and comforted me. I guess I calmed down eventually. I stayed with them a little longer after that.

Life Isn't Always a Bowl of Cherries

I turned 21 on the day we buried my dad so that night Ann and I went to the bar. We had a good time until we went to the 49er after the bar closed, and we got into a fight over some guy. The next day I went back to her house and my aunt told me I couldn't come back because I got in a fight with Ann. I guess I must have beat her up. That's why they didn't want me there. So I went back to my old self again, staying here and there.

After that I left Dulce again.

LIFE ON THE STREET

I had gone to Albuquerque with my cousins to get some stuff. It was night when we got there so we got a room. One of my cousins was taking acid and he offered some to us, so I tried it. It made me see things that were not real. I guess I had my cousin running all over the motel. I told him a black guy had a gun which I guess was not true but I was really tripping. The next day they were ready to go back to Dulce, but I didn't want to go back. I guess I wanted to try out street life. So they went back and I just stayed in Albuquerque. I met all kinds of people. I met this one lady, her name was May. She was tall, white and had black curly hair. She was a lot older than me. She was probably old enough to be my mother. But she was a nice friend to hang with. One time we met these guys. They were friendly and they invited us to their house. We went there and partied with them. They were nice, I forgot their names. We would just hang around down town with all the rest of the street people. It was kind of fun and I would stay anywhere I could. Then one night I was walking through Central Park. There was a black guy sitting on the bench and he asked me if I wanted a drink. So I said ok. Then we started talking and I ended up drinking with him all night. He told me his name was Jordan and he worked at Sambo's. After that I started hanging with him. He had a white friend who didn't like me. I guess I interfered with their friendship but I didn't care. I would wait for Jordan to get off work. This one time we slept in an abandoned house, his friend and us. We got up early. The next day I was wondering where did they get Kentucky chicken from? Then I finally snapped: the dumpster. I couldn't believe it. I am glad they didn't offer me any. After that I just hung around with them. Later on we started hanging with a different guy, his name was Sam, an older, tall black man. I don't know how old he was, I never asked. Anyway, we hung around the streets and slept in abandoned houses. Then one day Jordan told Sam he didn't want to keep letting me sleep in abandoned houses. So when he got paid he got us a place on Center Street. It was a nice room, enough for one bed and bathroom. We all stayed there. Sam slept on the floor. One night Jordan broke his leg so we went to the hospital and they had to keep him there. The next day Sam and I went to visit him. I had a bottle of Vodka in my bag. So we gave him some in a cup. We visited for a while then Sam and I left and went to the park. We traded some vodka with two white guys for a couple of pills. I don't know what kind of pills they were but the next thing I knew I woke up in the hospital. When they let me out of the hospital it was already dark. I was crossing the street when this lady hit me. I flew up in the air and landed on the sidewalk. I ended up right back in the hospital. This time they called a taxi to take me home. The next day Sam told me I almost hit the bench. I told him I didn't remember anything. We went to the hospital and told Jordan what happened. He got worried and checked out so he could take care of me. The next day I saw my sister Frankie and Alex walking down the sidewalk so I called to them. They told me they had come looking for me. All four of us hitched a ride to Dulce. Jordan and I stayed in Dulce for a while. We bought a car from a guy and used it until it broke down, then Jordan burned it and we went back to Albuquerque. After that he wanted to go to Phoenix, so we hitched to Phoenix. We stayed with his aunt for a while, then we stayed with his mom and his little brother Ice. One time we were going somewhere with Jordan's friend in his car. I didn't know where we were going or what we were going to do. It was dark, and we pulled up to some building. Jordan and his friend told me to stay in the car. The next thing I knew there were cops behind us. They arrested us and we went to jail. The next day they let me go so I had to walk from the jail all the way to his mother's house which was a long way. When I got there his mother got mad because Jordan was still in jail. She told his uncle "I want that Mexican out of my house". She was referring to me. His brother Ice said to just ignore her. Then here comes Jordan. He got out. Then everything went back to normal again. Until one night Jordan found Ice's joints. There was a lot in a bag. So he took it and we ended up in Tucson Arizona down the main street. He saw this guy in a long coat. He told me let me see if I can sell him some joints! I told him no because he looks like an undercover cop! But he didn't listen to me and the next thing I knew we were going to jail. I ended up in a big cell with a lot of ladies. I really didn't talk to anyone much. I stayed there for two weeks and then Jordan and I went to court and they let us go. We started hitching back to Phoenix. This hippie couple picked us up and they were talking to Jordan. They wanted us to go with them to their house and drink with them and take nude pictures, and they would pay us fifty dollars. I told Jordan I didn't want to do that. He got upset with me all the way back to his mother's house. When we got there he was really mad. He started beating on me and then he threw me out at night time.

 I didn't know where to go so I ended up downtown. I slept in the bus station. I guess some girl took my nice black velvet blazer and gave me an ugly green jacket. Well anyway that's what I woke up with the next morning. I had no place to go so I just ended up hanging around down town with the rest of the bums. I didn't know what to do. Then one day Jordan's little brother Ice told me a check had come for me but they sent it back to the post office. So him and his friend took me to the post office and I got it. Then I went to the bank and cashed it. After that they took me to a hotel to pick up my stuff I had left there. As soon as I got out of the car Ice grabbed my money out of my pocket and they took off. The landlord got their license plate and I called the police. I went with the police until we found where that guy's house was. I got some of my money back. After that I got off downtown and got me a place to stay. It was a nice room. I don't remember how long I stayed there but it was nice. After that Jordan caught up with me and my friends. We were getting ready to jump the train to New York but I ended up going with Jordan again. I don't know why I kept going back to him. He didn't care about me.

Then one day we got stopped by the cops and they asked us our names. I lied about my name and social security number and they let me go but they took Jordan to jail. I didn't know what to do after that. I got drunk with his cousin James and his friends. That night I ended up in Las Vegas. Of course I didn't know what to do but walk the streets.

I walked to a place where the soup line was. I was really yelling and asking the people who were waiting to eat "Does anyone want to hitchhike with me to Phoenix?" I kept saying it over and over until this one black guy said "I'll go". He was short and had an afro, a little taller than me. He told me his name was Bill. Instead of hitching back to Phoenix we just started drinking and stayed at an abandoned house. After that I just hang around the street with different people. Then one day I was walking by the train tracks and I heard someone say "Do you still want to hitch back to Phoenix?" It was Bill. I said yes. So we started hitching to Phoenix. We got there at night so we just slept by some church.

Then one day we were sitting by the park and the police were walking around asking people their names. They came to us and I told them the truth, my name was Sireana Atole. Then they arrested me. When you first get there they put you in a big cell with the rest of the people. I met this lady named Candy. She was white, short, had curly hair to her shoulders and small. Anyway we stayed in that cell for a while, like a week. Anyway it felt like a week. After that they took us to the main side where the doors slam. When you first get in there they give you a blue outfit and shoes. After that they take you to get a spray down then you shower. After that you go in a cell with other inmates. I really didn't talk to anyone. I met this one Indian lady at lunch whose name was Jane. She told me she was in there for killing. She traded me my cookies for some cigarettes. After lunch you go back to your cell.

Candy got out so I met another lady name Terry. She was white. Then one day it was visiting hour they called me and I went to the room where you talk through the window on a phone. It was Bill. He asked me how long I would be in. I told him I didn't know. Anyway he put some money in my commacertz, so I bought me cigarettes and stuff I needed. Then one day during lunch time this white girl told everyone "Don't mess with her" (meaning me). "She is Apache Indian I heard they are mean and crazy". After she said that everyone just kept away from me. I guess they believed her. This was funny to me. It was funny because one day during lunch hour I guess everyone ran out of cigarettes and I was the only one that still had some. Anyway we were eating. It started from one table to the table I was on. This one girl she wanted to borrow two cigarettes from me. I didn't know her. Anyway it went from one ear to another until it got to Terry. She told them "ask her yourself". So after lunch that girl asked me if she could borrow two cigarettes. I gave them to her.

I knew I wouldn't get them back but I didn't care. Then one day they said Sireana Atole roll it up. I was glad I was getting out. I gave my candy and shampoo and conditioner to the ladies in the cell. Then Bill brought me some clothes but the pants were too big. So we took it back and got a smaller size. After that we went to the park. There were people drinking in a crowd so we joined them. The next thing I knew someone was calling me. It was Jordan. So, I left with him. I don't know what happened to Bill.

The same thing over again. Hanging around drinking with people. Then one day we hitched back to Dulce. We stayed with my family here and there. Then me and Jordan moved in with my sisters at the blue house.

I babysat my sister's little boy while she was at work. My younger brother Jr. used to come by and take us fishing or hunting. One time I guess I got drunk and I couldn't get into the house so I passed out on the porch. My brother Jr. was bringing my sister home, he told her "where did you get your new watch dog from". They started laughing and it was me, passed out on the porch. It was fun when he used to come around. He lived in Farmington , had a wife and three little girls at the time.

He used to try and sober me up. But I have such a hard head it was hard for him. But he did the best he could.

Anyway, he was younger than me. He was an out-going person who loved hunting, fishing and riding in the country. One time Jr. took Jordan and me hunting with him. We had to get up early at 4:00AM so we got ready and it was still dark outside. We went out to the woods and we got ready to eat our eggs and we found out we had no salt. They don't taste good without salt. Anyway, he and Jordan went hunting on foot. I stayed in the blazer and waited for them.

Then I looked out the window, here comes Jr. with blood on him. I thought he got hurt, but he got his deer. He told me "you should have seen Jordan he was doing his jungle dance". I guess Jordan had never seen anything like that before. He could not stop talking about it. Anyway, I was glad he enjoyed it.

Jordan started drinking and hanging around with other ladies. Then one night I went with my cousins to a party. The next day I got home and found out that Jordan left. He took everything: the car, my sister's TV, stereo, and my jewelry, and went back to Albuquerque. I never saw him again, after all that.

One day my sister and I went to town. We met R.T. and his friend standing by the store. I told R.T. to go with me to the Inn to my friend's room so I could pawn her my bracelets then we went back to the house. That's the first time I met R.T.. We started going together but it was pretty off and on. We really didn't have a place to go so we would sleep anywhere we could. R.T. always had a sleeping bag, even in the winter time we would sleep in the snow with a sleeping bag. I used to drink a lot. I would end up in jail or detox. Later I went to treatment centers which didn't do any good. I would come home and end up doing the same things over again. Sleep anywhere, end up in jail or detox, on probation. One time R.T. and I were drinking at my cousin's house. I don't know what happened but I guess I hit R.T. in the eye and the next thing I know he hit me in the eye. We both had black eyes. We didn't care we went to the bar and ordered our drinks. The bartender asked us what happened, we told her what happened and we all just laughed about it. It was funny.

A NEW BEGINNING

Then one day tribal housing told R.T. they had a house for us. it was in Rivertown behind my sister's house. We had nothing so my sisters gave us some furniture, so did his brother. It was a nice apartment. Of course, we kept drinking and ended up in trouble.

A lot of times we would sober up. I even tried getting my GED and working at detox but it didn't work. I only lasted for a while and I would end up drinking again.

One morning it was so funny. R.T. was up building a fire and I guess it would not start so he got the rubbing alcohol and put some in the fire and I guess it blew up in his face and he was really smoking. His hair was smoking and his eyebrows were burnt. It was so funny we could not stop laughing. After all that the fire burned good.

We kept on drinking a lot and ending up in jail. People would come over and drink with us. It seems like every chance we got we would get drunk. It's hard to write about things you did when you were drinking because it's hard to remember.

Then one day I guess my drinking made me turn yellow. I didn't want to go to the hospital but my sister and her husband finally took me to the Indian Hospital in Santa Fe. I stayed there for a while before they let me go. R.T. was there too, but he left before me. We both decided that we didn't want to drink anymore. I got scared of it. So, I told myself "I am not drinking no more".

Our lives changed a lot. One night I was at his sister's house and she told me "you and R.T. have been together for a long time. Have you ever thought of marrying him?" I told her no I never thought of that. So one day R.T. and I were in the living room and I told him what his sister said to me. I guess he thought about it then he proposed to me in the living room.

After that we started getting things ready for our big day. We went to Farmington to get everything we needed for a wedding. My sister-in-law got the cake. My family and cousins did the cooking. My brother-in-law from Laguna gave me away. R.T.'s best man was his brother. It was at the Reform Church. There were a lot of people. Some I didn't even know. Afterwards we went outside to take pictures. It was raining that day. It was the most happiest day for me. Everything went great on that day July 10, 1999. I was 39 years old when we got married.

After all that we just lived a normal life. Then one day we were going to the casino down south. I was looking at R.T. smoking a joint. I asked him what does that do to you, he said it gets you feeling good. So I said let me try it. It made me feel good and I started laughing and having a good time. After that day I started smoking. I guess I liked the feeling. I used to smoke a lot and even smoked everyone else's bag. They used to hide their bags from me. They used to say "here she comes hide your bag or she'll smoke it all".

It was fun to smoke. My husband and I would go to the casino down south and we would be all high. I think the people that work there knew we were high but never said anything to us. I guess because we never caused trouble or anything. We used to just play the slot machines and enjoy ourselves. One time we were there and my sister called me over. I went to her and she look at me and said you're high? I started laughing and she said you're high. After that my husband and I still went there high or not. I keep smoking. Then one night we were coming back from Ignacio and I told him I don't want no more. I would quit for a while then I would start again. Then one day I tried cocaine. I liked it but afterwards I guess I was taking too much. I got to a point where I couldn't sleep and then one night we went to Ignacio to see R.T.'s friend. He got some for R.T.. We took some and we were smoking weed too. We stayed there for a while then we left. On the way home I told R.T. I don't want no more. So after that I quit coke. Which was good because I don't know how to do coke. I wanted more when I was already feeling good. I was one of those people who wanted more even though you are high you still want more. So I was glad I quit.

I kept smoking weed until one day I didn't like it no more so I quit smoking.

After I quit smoking R.T. kept smoking but I didn't mind. Later on I got me a job at the dorm as a cook. I worked there for almost two years. It was ok, I got along with everybody except the boss. I got into an argument with him twice when I was working. He would really argue. We would both would yell really loud at each other until one of us gave up. Then I would go back to work like nothing happened, it was funny. Then one day I quit and got a different job which was at the GED building. Instead of working, I was working on getting my GED. Then I went for the test in Farmington, NM. I didn't pass one, but I passed two. So I just gave up. After that I quit working for a while, then later on I got a job again but this time it didn't last long because my leg started acting up. I quit trying to work because my arthritis got worse and it was hard to walk.

After that I just stayed home with my husband and my Chihuahua puppies. I loved my Chihuahuas. The first one I got was

"Two-Bits". She was so tiny and cute I used to always tell her say mama. Then one day I was going to the casino. I told R.T. to drop me off there. When I was getting off I heard someone say mama. I turned around and I asked R.T. "did she just say mama?" and he said yes. I was really surprised. I could not believe it. The next time was down south at the other casino. Same way, I got off and she said mama again. After that I never heard her say it again. But she was a smart dog and still is. Then came Black Jack. He was my baby. He's the only one that wore clothes and loved to act baby to me. He was also very protective of me. The rest were just normal puppies.

2-bits is the best one. When she was small, she would eat sunflower seeds and pinions. She just knew where they were in my purse. She would scratch on my purse until she would unzip it, then I would give her a pinion or sunflower seed and she would crack it open and eat the inside. She really enjoyed it. There were a lot of things she did that would make you laugh. One time my sister Fran came over and I was sitting at the table with 2-bits sitting across from me on the other side of the table. You should have seen the look on my sister's face! She looked shocked. I just started laughing. Well enough of 2-bits.

I think it was on July 8, 2016 when I had my hip surgery. I went to the hospital in Pagosa Springs CO for my surgery and my husband was with me. When they took me to my room after surgery R.T. was nowhere around. When he came to the room, I asked him "Where were you?" and he said he was outside waiting in the car. Then he made an excuse to leave, he said he had to get home to feed the puppies. I just told him to go ahead. I stayed in the hospital.

Later on, my best friend came over to see me. She brought me some coloring books and a reading book. Her name is Val. She is a tall, white lady, really fun to be with. She makes me laugh because she has such a weird, loud laugh.

I met her when my thyroid got really bad. The doctor said if I did not go in it could have killed me. So, I ended up in the hospital for a while, then when I came home Val was the one to draw my blood a few times. Then one day she asked me if I would like to go with her to Farmington to go shopping, and I said OK. So, we went shopping on a Saturday. It was fun. She brought her son. After that we just became friends. She was a field nurse who worked in Dulce. Later on, she resigned and got married and lives in Pagosa Springs. We still keep in touch. I call her my sister and she call me her sister.

The other people that came to see me was my best friend Mar, and my niece Tash, and her husband and daughter. They brought me flowers which was nice of them to do.

I talked with the people at the hospital about putting me in the rehab center to help me get therapy on my legs. It sounded good at the time, but later on I changed my mind. I called my sister and told her I didn't want to go to the rehab center. She said she had an extra room I could use and stay with her. But the man that worked at the hospital said they already made the arrangement. My sister tried to talk for me, but it was no use. So, I went to a rehab place near Farmington NM.

I got settled in and my sisters left. I asked Fran if she would come visit me, she said they would. It was a lie because I called and asked her if she was coming to visit me and all she did was laugh at me. That hurt me but I just told myself "I guess they don't care for me".

My older sister Dar did come to see how I was doing. It was nice for them to come by. I was glad she came because it made me feel like she cared for me, and I was thankful for that.

It was not really lonely because my husband would come see me every day. He would bring me clean clothes and something to eat from Sonya's, or things I needed. He would check me out on weekends when we did not have physical therapy to take me home to see my puppies.

It was OK. I got along with everybody, the nurses, the staff, and the patients.

The nurses and therapists used to kiss me on the cheek. R.T. and I met this one nurse, she was really nice. She would come into my room and sit on my bed and tell me something she did that was funny. Her name was Nancy, she was nice, and fun. I also met a lot of nice workers there, old and young and they all treated me pretty good.

Except one therapist named Bill. He didn't like anyone who came in. After awhile we started to talk a little bit until he made me mad. Bill had heard the worker ask me if I wanted to take a shower and I said ok. She helped me get in the shower and I was sitting in there when Bill came in. I had nothing to cover me with, so she gave me a hand towel which was not big enough to cover me up. I was surprised and shocked because he was looking right at me. When he left, I asked the worker if it was ok for Bill to just come in like that and she said yes. To me it didn't feel right but I did not say anything. After that I just went back to my room and I watched "I Love Lucy" for the rest of the day.

The next time it was during therapy. The ladies were trying to help me walk on the bars and Bill came over to help and he put his hand on my butt. I got mad and was asking myself "Why is he touching my butt?" I thought they were not supposed to do that. But I guess they do anything they want.

So, I stayed there a little longer. Then my husband took me to Pagosa Springs CO to see my doctor, and the doctor gave me permission to leave the rehab center. So, we went back to the rehab. It was raining so I waited in the car and R.T. went in and got all my stuff and we went back home to Dulce.

But things were not the same. R.T. changed. He started putting me down all the time, and making me feel like I was nothing. I started to give up on everything I was doing. He made me feel so hopeless that I would just stay in my room and cry. I felt like he did not care for me anymore.

Ever since I got Rheumatoid arthritis it ruined me pretty bad. My body started to give up on me. First it was my hip then it went to my hands and they started hurting bad. One time I was trying to sort beans and they just went right through my hands. Then as it got worse my hands started to get deformed. My knee stiffened up on me and I tried everyway to straighten my knee but I could not.

Then my body was getting worse. I ended up in a wheelchair. I had to have my husband take care of me. He used to help me shower, braided my hair, and dressed me. He also made my meals for me. I mainly stayed in my room. Every time I wanted to go to the living room or kitchen, he would meet me by the door and ask me what I wanted. I would tell him and he would say "Go back to your room and I'll bring it to you". I always wondered why he would not let me in the kitchen or living room. I would ask myself "What is he hiding that he doesn't want me to see?" But I never asked him, I just kept it to myself.

I started to feel like he really didn't care for me anymore, like I was just in the way. But I never asked how he felt about me being in a wheelchair plus not being able to do anything. I think he felt like I was in the way but he would not say anything to me. When we would go out of town to Walmart or the other stores, he would put me in the aisles and tell me to wait there. I would sit there and wait for him. I know what he was up to. He used to look at the ladies, probably wishing he had one instead of me. It used to hurt but I just had to live with it, so I just let him do what he wanted. When we would go out of town, I just started telling him to go ahead inside and I would wait in the car. He would go in and take forever, then when he finally came out, he would just have 3 CD's. I'd say "Is that all you went in for?" and he wouldn't say anything, he would just smile that pretty smile, then we would head home.

We were the type that never stay home. We were always going someplace. Sometimes we would go out to the country for a ride. Sometimes when I had money, he would take me downtown to the casino. Sometimes he would get mad at me for wanting to go to the casino. I would say "why are you getting mad, I don't tell you to quit your smoking". We made an agreement: when I want to go to the casino I can go, and I don't say anything about his smoking.

Then the saddest part of our lives came, when my husband found out he had stage 4 cancer.

R.T.

Well, let me tell you about my husband. He was a Jicarilla Apache, half Laguna Pueblo. He was 57 years old when he died. Everybody called him Bob Marley. At first, I wondered why they called him that. Then one day when his sister called him that, I looked at him then looked at Bob Marley's picture then I saw the resemblance. I said to myself "they sure do look alike".

But my husband was a really nice person. Everybody liked him. He always helped people out. People were always happy to see him. He was always happy to see them. He would always shake their hands or say Hi. He always had a smile on his face.

He loved to exercise a lot. He loved to draw. He drew me a picture of Bob Marley, a picture of a Tiger, and some other ones. That was before he got really sick. He also loved to plant flowers and trees. Also, he like hunting for horns out in the woods. Sometimes we would go for a ride out to the lakes just to look at the eagles and hawks. Sometimes the cops would stop us and ask R.T. why we were always going out to the lakes. R.T. would say "to look at the eagles and hawks". They would look at us like we were crazy. But we were not crazy, we just loved to look at them. We thought they were the most beautiful birds.

One time we went out there for a ride, and I guess we both went to sleep. I woke up and we were driving off the road. I yelled

"R.T. we're off the road!" and he woke up and put us back on the road. He just smiled like he always does. Then we went home.

Those were some of the things he loved to do before he got cancer.

One day he started to lose his voice. He went to the clinic and they told him he had a sore throat. But he got worse. One evening I was watching TV in my room. He came down the hallway saying: "Bree I can't breathe" and he was hitting his chest. Then he kneeled in front of me and he said to me "Bree, I don't want to die". I called the EMT's. They came to check him and asked him if he wanted to go to the hospital. He did not want to, but I told him "You better go because if something happens, I can't help you". So, they took him to the hospital. They did not do anything for him, so we brought him back. He was ok for a while, but later on he got worse, so they flew him in a plane to Albuquerque.

The doctors in the hospital said his cancer was spreading and they had to operate. They kept him there for awhile before he came home. They had taken out his vocal-cord so he could not talk. We communicated with each other through paper and pen. Sometimes we would get mad at each other because I couldn't understand him and I would tell him to write it down. I did the best I could to understand him.

He had to go to chemotherapy in Farmington. I did not mind going with him to his treatments because when he would go in, I would call my niece Tosh, and she and her husband would pick me up. We would go to the casino and enjoy ourselves. When R.T. was finished, he would text me and we would go back and get him and we would head home.

First his treatments were every week, then every two weeks. I thought he was getting better, but I guess he was getting worse.

But before he got worse, we got to have our last Christmas together. I bought him a stereo, because he always wanted one. One thing about R.T., he was always happy with what he got. He bought me a nice record player, a salt and pepper shaker and tea pot with a cup. We both loved what we gave to each other on our last Christmas together.

We had a lot of fun together before he got worse. We used to go for rides to Chama to get groceries. Sometimes we would take his older brother with us to Pagosa Springs. R.T. would go real fast on the curves. I would tell him to slow down and he would just give me that big smile.

But we would get there safe and his brother would do his shopping while we waited in the car.

I told R.T. a story about when I was young; I was walking by Goodman's Store and I was not watching where I was going. I sure hit the parking meter with my face real hard. R.T. started laughing, but the sad part was he could not laugh like he wished he could. But I'm glad I could make him laugh anyway I could.

R.T. used to sleep in the living room. One time I told him to sleep with me. I had a canopy bed. He lay down by me. I could not hold him really good because of my arthritis, but I would try. He would just smile at me for trying. It didn't work out too well so he moved to the bedroom by mine. Every night before he went to bed, he would come in my room and kiss me on the forehead, like telling me good night.

I sure miss all those days. It's hard to write about the good times we had together but I am trying my best.

Then we started going to Albuquerque for his treatment. One day when we got there for his treatment, he was not feeling good so they put him in the hospital, and myself and his sister and her husband came home without him.

I went to my sister's house, Fran, and I stayed there with her and her family. One day I got a call from the social worker telling me they wanted a meeting with me and my husband's family.

I went to the meeting with my sister Fran and her son Dex. When we got there R.T. was sitting on his bed with that pretty smile. I couldn't hug him because I was in a wheelchair but between me and him, we have a handshake of our own we use. R.T. showed me a paper that said they were trying to put him in the old folks home. When the social worker came in with other people that worked there, I told them no, my husband is not going to an old folks home. R.T. also wrote on a piece of paper that he would like to die at home where he is comfortable. It made me cry knowing that I was losing him slowly.

My sister and I went out in the hall, and I told her I was going to need R.T.'s family to help me with him, since it is hard for me to do things. She told me I had to speak up and tell them that. So, we went back into the room and I told them. We talked about it and came to a solution. R.T.'s sister said she would make room for him in her house so he could stay there. She did not like the idea of him going to the old folks home either.

I went to my sister-in-law's house to stay with my husband. He was getting worse and he could no longer help me, so my sister-in-law started helping me with my bathing and fixing my hair.

I used to sit there and look at him, and wonder "Why God?" I got mad at God and asked "Why are you taking him away from me?

He is all I have. You know without him I will be lost". Also, I would sit by my husband and wonder what he was thinking. It was hard for us to tell each other what we were thinking because we never told each other how we felt. I wish we did but now it is too late. I know we had a lot of feeling for each other. I am glad I stayed with him through his last days, even though it was hard.

We still laughed together when he was not in pain. In the mornings he would watch me when I got up. I would bend really low to sit in the wheelchair and he would laugh and tell me that it looked like I was going to hit the floor. I would just start laughing too. One time I was sitting by the table looking at the catheter drainage container that was sitting on the floor. It had bloody stuff in it and it looked real gross. I was starting to want to throw up. R.T. saw me and he waved at his sister to show her what I was doing, then we all started laughing. I think that was the last time we laughed together.

I would ask my sister-in-law if she thought R.T. would ever get better. She would say "I don't know. We just have to wait and see". I already knew the answer, which I did not want to hear.

He kept going to treatment in Farmington, NM, which was doing him no good. He continued to get worse. I guess stage 4 cancer is pretty bad and it was spreading. R.T. told me it was getting worse, and I knew I was losing him.

One day he came home from Farmington and they had not been able to help him, so his nephew took him to the hospital in Pagosa Springs. The next day I was sitting in the living room when the phone rang and my sister-in-law answered it. I already knew it was bad news. I told her I didn't want to talk to anyone. I just sat there and started crying. I tried to call my sister Fran but couldn't reach her so I called my niece. I told her her uncle was dying in the hospital in Pagosa. She told me "Don't cry Bree". I told her I couldn't get in touch with her mom to tell her. Then I called my other sister Dora, and when I told her R.T. was dying, she asked me what happened. I thought she knew he had cancer but I guess not. Not many people knew about him. Like I said, we lived a private life.

After I finished on the phone, we got ready to go to Pagosa to the hospital. I had a hard time getting into the van but they got me in. When we got there, R.T.'s older brother was already there. I went in and sat down and listened to his brother talking to him. Then my sister Fran and my nephew Dex came in. They gave us the notebook he wrote in. I read it. He had put the Lord's Prayer on it and said his good byes to us. He said he loved us all. Also, he wanted to be cremated. His sister wanted the notebook, but I ended up with it, and I still have it.

My sister and I went to sit in the lobby and wait for Tash and her husband Del, and Shea. When they came, we all just sat there and talked for a while. Then Tash asked if I had had sometime with him by myself, and I said no. So, we all went back in there. Tash started to cry but she held it back and they all talked to R.T.. He had a smile on his face like he was happy to see them. They talked to him for the last time. Then they put the phone by his ear and my nephew B.A. said a prayer for him. Then Tash said "Let's let Bree have some time with him alone. I held my husband's hand and I told him I wish he didn't have to leave me, "What am I going to do without you? I will be lost. Who is going to be there to help me? You were all I had. But I will remember all the good times we had together. I'll never forget you. I love you so much but I have to let you go". I sat there and held his hand and cried. I wish I could have been able to see him when I was talking to him but I could not because I was in the wheelchair. But he probably heard everything I said.

R.T. Passed away that night. I went home with my sister and her son. It was the saddest night for me. I lost him, and we never had kids, so I was all alone. But I have 2 sisters who were there for me. After I lost him there were some things I had to do and they helped me. Even my nieces and nephews helped me through my hard times. Other people helped me out too. Thank you all for helping me through the saddest days of my life.

After R.T. passed, I stayed with Fran for a while. Later on, we got into an argument and she told me I was on my own. I thought about what she said about me being on my own. I asked myself why she would say that. I have been on my own almost all my life until I met my husband.

Anyway, I moved into the hotel since I had no place to go. I just knew this was going to happen. I guess I was prepared for it because it really didn't bother me.

So, I ended up staying at the hotel for awhile because my house was being worked on.

My niece was working with me, so she would come everyday except week-ends. It was still hard for me because I missed my husband so much. At night I would go back to my room and cry. I just could not accept it that my husband was gone. I would go to bed and hope that the next day would be a good day.

I got along with the people that worked in the hotel. There was this one young girl that worked there that became like my little buddy. She was so nice and helpful. She would French braid my hair and one time she polished my nails. Once I told her to play the song "I'll Never Love Another" by Johnny Harden. She did, and I sure started crying. She was sitting there looking at me and I told her that was my husband and my song. She didn't know what to do, so

I started laughing and she turned it off and told me 'No more sad songs", It was funny.

One time it was night and I asked her to take me back to my room. We got to the room and she opened the door, and while she was messing with the door I was waiting in the hallway. I happened to look down the hallway to the end and there were two glass doors. I was looking that way and I swear I saw my husband. He was dressed the way he always dressed, light blue shirt, light blue jeans. He walked by the glass doors, he didn't come in. I knew it was him. I did not get scared. I asked her if she saw the guy that went by, and she said no. I told her it was my husband. She looked at me like I was crazy. Anyway, I know what I saw.

You really can't do anything in a motel but watch TV or go to the casino. Sometimes I just sat in the lobby and watched everybody. Sometimes I gambled when I had money. Sometimes my sister Dora would be there and I would go and sit with her in the casino.

One day I was talking to one of the workers there and I told her I felt bad about my sister and not talking, so one of us came up with the idea for me to write Fran a letter, asking her to forgive me. So, I wrote Fran a letter, and my niece J.C, Fran's daughter, gave it to her. After that we became sisters again.

I still stayed at the Motel. I started feeling like I was at the Old Folks home because I could not go anywhere. Everyone I knew had a van or a truck, which I cannot get into. Some people would come up to me and ask if R.T. was really gone, and I would say yes. One lady told me it was hard for her husband to believe it. I guess he took it hard. I guess it was hard for a lot of people. But I told them all "Yes, he's gone". After that people stopped asking me, which was good.

My husband's last wish was for me to have a warm place to live. That's why they fixed up the house for me. When I went home, for some reason I felt really comfortable, like my husband was saying to me "Welcome home". I felt really good.

So now I am enjoying myself at home with my two dogs. I think of my husband everyday but I know he is still with me in my heart. He always will be.